D1408769

Me and My Pet
FISH

Christine Morley and Carole Orbell

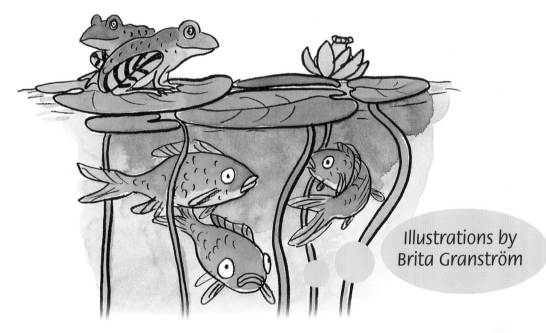

Illustrations by
Brita Granström

WORLD BOOK / TWO-CAN

First published in the United States and Canada by
World Book Inc.
525 W. Monroe
Chicago, IL 60661
in association with Two-Can Publishing Ltd.

For information on other World Book products, call 1-800-255-1750, x 2238.

Art director: Carole Orbell
Senior Managing Editor: Christine Morley
Designer: Lisa Nutt
Consultant: Lisa Cobb, Animal Nurse of the Year 1995
Illustrator: Brita Granström
Photographer: John Englefield
Special thanks to: Karen Ingebretsen, World Book Publishing

ISBN: 0-7166-1795-1 (hard cover)
ISBN: 0-7166-1796-X (soft cover)

Morley, Christine.
   Me and my pet fish / Christine Morley and Carole Orbell;
illustrations by Brita Granström.
       p. cm.
   Summary: A practical discussion of how to keep goldfish safely at home, what kind of environment to provide for them, what to feed them, and how to breed them.
   ISBN 0-7166-1795-1 (hardcover). -- ISBN 0-7166-1796-X (softcover)
   1. Goldfish--Juvenile literature. 2 Aquariums--Juvenile literature.
[1. Goldfish. 2. Aquariums. 3. Pets.] I. Orbell, Carole. II. Granström, Brita, ill. III. Title.
   SF458.G6M67 1997
   639.3'7484--DC21   96-50421

Printed in Hong Kong

1 2 3 4 5 6 7 8 9 10 01 00 99 98 97

Contents

Fishy friends

Goldfish make great pets. They are easy to keep and you'll have lots of fun watching them swim around. There's plenty to learn about these mini-pets, so keep on reading to find out how to be an expert fish keeper.

Is that me on the cover?

They're fintastic!

Goldfish are one of the easiest pets to take care of. They will be happy as long as their water is clean and they are fed regularly. They are a smart choice if your home is too small for other pets.

Fish are pets that everyone can enjoy.

In or out?

Goldfish like to live in cold water. This means they can be kept outside in a pond, or indoors in a special tank called an aquarium.

Cool customers

Although goldfish like cold water, other types of fish, such as tropical fish, live in warm water. This is because they come from hot countries where the water in ponds and streams is as warm as the water in your bath.

Hey, watch me dive!

Show-off.

Pond-watching is fun, especially on hot summer days.

Here comes my dinner!

Fish faces

When you first buy your goldfish, you might not be able to tell one from another. After a while, you will learn who's who and then you can give each one a name. Your goldfish won't know their names, but some can be trained to swim toward you when you whistle.

Learning about fish

Goldfish are special pets because, like all fish, they do not breathe air and can live only in water. To take good care of your goldfish, you need to learn a little about how they live underwater.

Super swimmers

Fish are great swimmers. The long, thin shape of their bodies helps them glide easily through water. They use their fins, which are pieces of skin shaped like triangles, to push themselves forward, to go up and down, and to stop.

Fish breathe underwater through their gills.

Care for a swim around the tank?

No thanks. I'm off to aquarobics.

Deep breathing

Just like people, fish need a special gas called oxygen to survive. Fish take their oxygen from water. They use a particular part of their body, called gills, to do this. Gills are covered by pieces of skin shaped like half circles. See if you can spot the gills on your fish, just behind their eyes.

Don't upset your fish with loud noises.

Eye spy

Take a peek at your goldfish. You will see that they don't have eyelids like us. This means that they can't shut their eyes to go to sleep. Instead, they rest by keeping still, with their eyes open, usually at the bottom of the tank.

Turn off the tank light at night so that your goldfish can rest.

Is it bedtime already?

Feeling sound

If you play your stereo very loud, you can often feel the noise because it makes the floor shake, or vibrate. Goldfish "hear" sounds by feeling vibrations in the water. Never tap on the side of your tank, as this could give your goldfish a nasty shock.

Really cool!

All fish are cold-blooded. This means that their bodies stay the same temperature as the water where they are swimming. If you put goldfish in warm water, they will get too hot. They may even die.

Water lilies make great sunshades for goldfish in outdoor ponds.

All shapes and sizes

Goldfish come in lots of amazing shiny colors—from gold and silver to red and black. Some goldfish have long, flowing fins, while others have big, bulging eyes!

I'm round, but lovely!

Tall tails

There are many different types of goldfish. Some, such as the common goldfish and the comet, have slim bodies and single tails. Others, such as fantails and moors, have round bodies and two tail fins.

This is the common goldfish.

A fantail has two tail fins.

I'm a speedy comet.

A shubunkin has brown and gray splotchy skin.

Moors are jet black and have eyes that stick out.

Bubble trouble

Some goldfish look very strange. They have eyes that stick out from the sides of their heads. These goldfish, called bubble eyes, have huge sacks of water under their eyes. The heavy sacks stop bubble eyes from swimming properly.

Fancy fins

All goldfish have fins at the top and bottom of their bodies. Some varieties, such as fantails, have very long fins that trail behind them as they swim. These long fins look very pretty, but they also slow down the fish.

A beautiful goldfish may win a prize at a show.

I think he likes me.

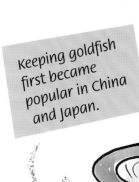

Keeping goldfish first became popular in China and Japan.

Crazy colors

Most goldfish are beautiful, bright, and shiny. But they all have a very dull-looking ancestor, a gray fish called the Crucian carp. It was from this type of carp that people in China and Japan first began to breed goldfish.

Are you ready?

Before you buy goldfish, you will need to make them a home. All you need is a fish tank and a few pieces of equipment.

When choosing equipment, ask for advice in a pet store.

Tank talk

Remember that the bigger the tank, the more fish it can hold. To keep six fish, you need a tank that is 36" long, 13" wide, and 16" deep (90cm long, 38cm wide and 30cm deep). You can keep two or three fish in a tank that is 16" long, 12" wide, and 24" deep (45cm long, 30cm wide and 30cm deep). You will also need to buy a light and a lid to fit over the tank.

Blowing bubbles

To keep the water clean, you will need a filter and an air pump. A filter is a small machine that fits inside the tank. It catches bits of dirt and food floating in the water. An air pump moves the tank water around, which helps to keep it full of oxygen.

Your tank should have a cover to keep out dust – and nosy pets!

That big, furry thing is after us again!

Rocks and stones

Gravel and rocks make the tank more interesting to look at. Also, goldfish like to hide behind the rocks and nose around in the gravel, looking for food. *Always* use smooth gravel; goldfish can cut their mouths on sharp edges.

Make a pebble cave for your aquarium, using special glue from a pet store.

Paint a bright background and tape it behind your aquarium.

Underwater gardens

You can buy plants to grow in water. They look pretty, and fish like to dart in and out of the leaves. Some like to nibble on them, too. You can also buy plastic plants that look like the real thing, but don't taste as good!

Water work

Goldfish are very particular about their homes. To keep them happy, their water must be clean, fresh, and just the right temperature.

Tap danger
Before you fill your tank, the water must be treated with a special liquid called a dechlorinator. This is because tap water contains a chemical, called chlorine, that is harmful to fish. You can buy dechlorinators from a pet store.

Tap water needs treating before it's safe for fish.

Water test
Goldfish can survive only in cool water. Keep a thermometer inside the tank and check it every day to make sure the water is not too hot or cold. The thermometer should read between 10 and 20°C (60 and 70°F).

Somebody, put the light on!

Too much algae can turn the water green.

Green scene
Sometimes you might find that the tank water has turned green. This is caused by tiny plants called algae. Algae also grow on the sides of the tank. But don't worry, they don't harm fish. In fact, fish like to eat algae! Find out how to get rid of excess algae on page 23.

Gasping goldfish

If you put too many fish in the tank, they will have problems getting enough oxygen. Keep a close watch on your fish. If lots of them come to the surface, opening their mouths and gasping for air, you have a problem.

Phew! It's like sardines in here!

Air rescue!

To add oxygen to your tank, take out some old water and add fresh water at the right temperature. Find out how to do this on page 22. If the fish are still gasping, you have too many fish for that size tank.

Splash down!

Now that you know what equipment you need, you can set up your aquarium. Ask an adult to help you. Remember to wear old clothes, in case you get wet!

An adult should set up the light, pump, and filter.

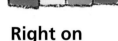

Right on

First, decide where to put your tank. Remember, when it's full of water it may be too heavy to move! Put it on a sturdy, even surface, away from anything hot, such as a sunny window or a radiator. Make sure that it's near an electrical outlet.

Clean and dry

Dilute one tablespoon of salt into half a liter (1 pint) of warm water. Use this to rinse your tank, then wipe it dry with a clean cloth. Never use soap or disinfectar these are dangerous to fish.

Things seem to be going downhill!

Don't put your tank in a hot place, or on electrical equipment.

Watch out for crooked shelves!

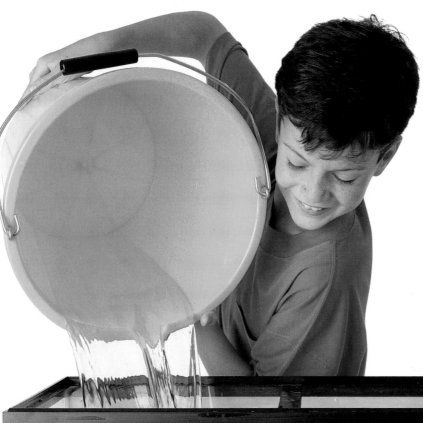

Wash and rinse
Before putting in the gravel, rinse it a few times to remove any dust and dirt. Then pour it into the tank, making it deeper at the back. If you have any rocks, thoroughly scrub them in warm salt water.

Water world!
Tape your painted background onto the back of the tank, and put a thermometer inside the tank. Now fill the tank about one-third full with dechlorinated water, ready for planting.

To avoid messing up the gravel, put a plate on top of it and pour the water onto the plate.

Plant power

Plants are your fish's friends. They give shade and shelter, as well as providing food. Real plants also help keep the water full of oxygen.

Going green

You can buy real or plastic plants for your tank. Whichever you choose, make sure that you buy them from an aquarium or a pet store. Remember that you may have to replace real plants often, if your goldfish eat them.

Goldfish love playing hide-and-seek in the plants.

I look lovely against green!

Plants help to show off a goldfish's shiny scales.

I like a few leaves between meals.

Ship ahoy!
If you want, you can add a plastic ornament, such as a deep-sea diver or a shipwreck. Make sure that these are made especially for aquariums; some plastic toys are harmful to fish.

When you finish decorating your tank, ask an adult to turn on the pump, filter, and light. Now let your aquarium settle for a week before adding fish.

Ornaments are fun, but leave some room for your fish to swim around.

How to plant
Wash all your plants in salt water before planting them. This helps to get rid of pests and diseases. Make a hole in the gravel for each plant, just deep enough so that the roots fit snugly. Push the gravel back on top of the roots to hold the plant in place.

Rock garden
When all your plants are in place, add rocks, pushing them down firmly into the gravel so that they won't fall over. Now fill the tank with dechlorinated water, until the water almost reaches the top.

This is my home, not a toy box!

Going fishing

Most pet stores have hundreds of goldfish for you to choose from. Make sure you pick happy, healthy fish by following these tips.

There isn't much room in here.

Good goldfish
Healthy fish have a bright color, and they should be busy swimming around the tank. Watch out for fish that don't move a lot, as they could be sick. Check that their tails and fins are not damaged or drooping.

Take your new fish home quickly—it won't be very happy in a plastic bag.

The best place to buy fish is from a local aquarium shop or pet store.

Big or small?
Goldfish don't like to be alone, so it's best to buy two or three at first. Try to buy ones of the same size and type. If you put large and small fish together, the bigger ones might just swallow the smaller ones!

Home time

When you buy your goldfish, the clerk will put them in a plastic bag for you to take home. Once you're home, you will need to get the fish used to the water in the aquarium. Float the plastic bag in the water for 20 minutes. This should make the water temperature in the bag the same as that in the tank.

Use a thermometer to check the temperature.

Swimming free

Carefully open the bag, scoop some water from the tank, and add it to the bag. This way, the fish will become used to the tank water. Now gently tip the bag and let the fish swim out. Leave the filter and air pump on, but turn the light off, so the fish can rest.

Dinner time

To keep your goldfish in fine condition, you must give them the right food. Feed them once or twice a day, but don't overfeed—the water will start to smell!

Watch out for bigger fish taking all the food.

Please save some for us!

Dried food
The easiest type of food to give your goldfish is dried flakes, tablets, or pellets from a pet store. These have all the vitamins and minerals your fish need.

Check the label to make sure the food you buy is especially for goldfish.

Fast fleas and wiggling worms
Goldfish love a regular treat of live food, such as water fleas, called daphnia, and tubifex worms. You can buy these at a pet store, along with special worm feeders to put in the tank. As the worms wiggle through the feeder, the fish gobble them up!

How much food?
Start by giving your goldfish a pinch of food every morning. If they don't eat this all up in five minutes, give them less next time. Feed them live food, such as daphnia or tubifex, about once a week.

Warning – overfeeding!

You will soon learn when you have been overfeeding: your fish will leave their food. This food will start to rot, which turns the water cloudy and makes it smell. If this happens, cut down on feeding and scoop out uneaten food with a net.

Vacation time

You won't need to worry about your fish when you go on a short vacation. All you have to do is put a special block of dried food in the tank. This will release bits of food every day while you are away.

Bring me back some rocks!

Fish are pets you can leave safely for a short time.

I like to start the day with fish flakes.

Fish will swim to the surface when you feed them.

Aquarium care

Keeping your aquarium clean and fresh is part of the fun of looking after goldfish. Set aside a little time each week for this very important job.

Check list

You should check your aquarium every day. Make sure the filter, air pump, and light are working, and that the water temperature is right. If it's too cool, add dechlorinated warm water. If it's too warm, add some ice cubes in a plastic bag until it cools enough, then remove them.

Weekly work

Once a week, replace a little tank water, about 2 to 4 inches (5 to 10 cm), with clean, dechlorinated water. You can do this with a long, thin tube, called a siphon, which sucks out the water. Use the siphon to suck out bits of dirt on the gravel, too. Remember to switch off the pump, filter, and light before you begin.

Your fish can stay in the tank while you are siphoning.

Use a special scraper to get rid of algae.

Now and then

Ask a grown-up to check the air pump and change the filter every two to three weeks. You can also give the filter a good scrub with a brush and rinse it in clean water, but never use soap or disinfectant. If there's too much algae in your tank, use a special scraper to clean it off the sides.

Do I get a haircut, too?

A complete change

Once or twice a year you should clean the whole aquarium. Fill a plastic bucket with water from the aquarium and carefully put your fish in it. Rinse the gravel and wash all the plants in fresh water. Then replant the plants in clean gravel. Refill the tank with dechlorinated water that's the right temperature. Switch on the pump, light, and filter, then put the fish back.

Wear rubber gloves when you put your hands in a fish tank.

Snip, snip!

Keep your live plants healthy by cutting off dead leaves with a pair of scissors. Also, you might need to trim off the tops if the plants are growing too big for the tank.

Perfect ponds

Some types of goldfish are happy to live outside in a pond—even in winter. As well as being a perfect home for fish, a pond will attract lots of other creatures too, such as frogs, birds, and snails.

Dig deep

Your pond should be at least 18 inches (45 cm) deep. This is so the water at the bottom will not freeze in winter. Make it as big as possible—10 feet (3 meters) long is a good size. Line it with heavy plastic or rubber, which you can buy from a garden center.

Tough types

Single-tailed goldfish, such as common goldfish and comets, can live in ponds all year around. You can keep some relatives of goldfish, such as carp, in ponds too. You will find that outdoor goldfish grow bigger than those kept in an aquarium.

Digging a pond is hard work, so ask for lots of grown-up help!

I would help, but I'm not very good at digging!

Even shallow ponds can be dangerous if you fall in. Always have an adult with you.

Summer snacks

Make sure your pond fish get enough vitamins and minerals by feeding them pellets once a day. Never feed pond fish in winter, though. This is because they are hibernating, or resting, at the bottom of the pond.

Pond care

In summer, you may need to add more water to your pond. In the fall, you should clear out any fallen leaves or dead plants. When winter comes, float a large ball in the pond. If the pond freezes, ask an adult to lift the ball out to leave an air hole for the fish. Never break the ice; this can harm fish.

Some plants like to grow in shallow water at the pond's edge. Others grow in deeper water.

Checkup

If you take good care of your goldfish, they should stay healthy. If they do become sick, though, they will need your help to get better.

Feeling bad

You can often spot a sick goldfish by the way it moves slowly or lies at the bottom of the tank. Its fins droop and it may look very fat or very thin. Any fish that is behaving strangely should be put in a separate tank where you can keep a close eye on it.

Healthy fish never miss a meal!

In the net

To put your sick fish in a separate tank, you first have to catch him! Be patient. Gently put the net in the tank and move it toward the fish. A flick of the net should capture it. Cover the top of the net with your hand to stop the fish from jumping out.

Be careful when catching fish—you can easily scare them.

Fish hospital

A spare tank makes an excellent fish hospital. Decorate it with plastic plants and a small flowerpot on its side where the fish can take shelter. Keep any sick fish in the tank for a couple of weeks, until you are sure they are well again.

Does he have fleas too?

Use a small tank to carry your fish to the vet.

Getting better

To find out what is wrong with your fish, talk to a vet or someone who raises fish. Sometimes they can tell what is wrong from the way you describe your fish's problem. At other times, you might have to take your fish to the vet. He or she may give you medicine to put in the water to help your goldfish get better.

Fungus and spots

Goldfish can get white furry stuff, called fungus, growing on their bodies. Fungus is often caused by the fish living in a dirty tank.

Another common fish illness is called white spot. Lots of tiny white specks appear all over the fish's body and fins. Fungus and white spot can be treated by putting medicine in the water. Your vet will tell you how to do this.

Breeding fish

Goldfish are one of the easiest fish to breed. But although they lay hundreds of eggs, only a few baby fish survive to become fully grown.

Breeding time

Goldfish breed during spring and summer, when the weather is warm. You can tell when they are ready to breed, because the females have round, fat tummies that are full of eggs. Male goldfish get white spots all around their gill covers.

We're frying tonight!

When a male goldfish is ready to breed, he chases the female around the tank. The female releases hundreds of eggs that stick to plants. This is called spawning. Then the male squirts a liquid called milt over the eggs to make them hatch into baby fish, called fry.

Spawning fish are easy to spot because they chase each other around the tank.

We're making a big splash!

Hatching the eggs

Check your aquarium every day for eggs. They look like tiny spots of clear jelly stuck to plants. When the eggs appear, you should remove the parent fish, or they will eat the eggs. After five days the eggs will hatch and in a few more days the tiny fish will start swimming.

I can't wait till I'm older and golder.

These fry are around three months old. It can take a year for them to turn gold.

First swim

When the fry first hatch, they get their food from the egg sack in which they were born. When this is used up, you should feed them special fry food from an aquarium shop.

Put the parents in a separate tank or they'll eat the eggs.

Growing up

As the fry grow, put them into a larger tank. You will also have to give away or throw away many of the smaller ones to let the others grow strong and healthy. Use a cup to scoop up the fry—never use a net because this can damage them.

Community tanks

An aquarium that holds many different types of fish is called a community tank. When you have some experience caring for fish, why not set up your own community tank?

Happy families

For a community tank to be successful, all the fish must be happy to live in the same water temperature and like the same food. They must also have peaceful natures, or they could fight each other.

I like to swim near the surface to catch insects.

Expert choice

Choosing fish that like to live together is a job for someone who knows a lot about fish. It is best to ask a fish breeder or go to a pet store for advice.

Top to bottom

In most community tanks, the fish live at all levels, so they do not fight for food. Some will like to swim near the surface, others will stick to the middle level, and some will prefer to live near the bottom, grazing on the gravel.

You can set up a community of fish in an aquarium or in a pond.

Useful words

air pump A machine that moves water around in an aquarium. This helps to add oxygen to the water.

algae Tiny plants that grow in water. Too much algae will turn the tank water green.

breed A particular type of fish, such as a common goldfish or a comet. Also, when fish breed, it means that they have babies, or fry.

chlorine This is a chemical found in tap water that is harmful to fish. You can use a special liquid, called a dechlorinator, to make the tap water safe.

daphnia Tiny creatures, also called water fleas, that live in water. They are an excellent food for goldfish.

filter This helps to keep the tank water clean by catching pieces of dirt and food floating in the water.

fin This is a thin piece of skin on a fish's body that helps it move forward, stay upright, and stop in the water.

fry The name for baby fish.

gills Part of a fish's body that takes oxygen from water. Gills are just behind the fish's eyes and are covered by semi-circular flaps of skin.

hibernate This is something that fish do when the weather becomes cold. They become sleepy and do not move until the weather warms up.

milt Liquid that is squirted over fish eggs by male fish. This makes the eggs hatch into fry.

scales Thin, bony plates that cover the body of a fish.

tubifex Tiny worms that fish like to eat.